AT MALDON

'Eyesharp and utter and visceral, so s
lyrical: this is a stunning old-new po
– Kevin Crossley-Holland

'This is a glorious piece of writing. It's vivid. It's witty. It's delicate. It's masterfully paced. It sings.' – Helena Nelson, Happen*Stance*

'Inventive, striking and memorable. And a reminder that Morgan is one of the most original poets around.'
– Andrew Motion, *Guardian* 'Books of the Year'

J. O. Morgan lives in Scotland. *Assurances* (Cape, 2018), his narrative poem about the Cold War, won the 2018 Costa Poetry Award.
For the essay by Seth Insua from which the the back cover quotes, see www.asymptotejournal.com/criticism/j-o-morgan-at-maldon.

Praise for *Natural Mechanical* (Aldeburgh First Collection Prize):

'Remarkable. A gem of a poem' – Simon Armitage

'So vivid it is clearer than prose. If those who never touch poetry tried a few pages of this, they might become converts.'
– Rosemary Goring, *Herald*

'A literally fabulous achievement.' – *Times Literary Supplement*

Praise for *Long Cuts* (Scottish Book Awards shortlist):

'*Long Cuts* is every bit as fine as *Natural Mechanical*, in some respects better: sharper descriptions, richer language, more assured versification. I loved it.' – Christopher Reid

also by J. O. Morgan

Natural Mechanical (CBe, 2009)
Long Cuts (CBe, 2011)
In Casting Off (HappenStance, 2015)
Interference Pattern (Cape, 2016)
Assurances (Cape, 2018)

AT MALDON

J. O. Morgan

CB editions

to Alexandra

First published in 2013
by CB editions
146 Percy Road London W12 9QL
www.cbeditions.com

Second impression, 2019

Printed in England by Imprint Digital, Exeter EX5 5HY

ISBN 978–0–9573266–5–1

ARGUMENT

An invading force. A local army mustered to defend. A
battle. An overwhelming loss. And, later, a poem.

A poem that, somewhere in the intervening thousand or
so years, loses its beginning and its end, but, nonetheless,
becomes the history it tries to tell.

An unreliable poem from a poet not permitted onto the
field, who has no immunity, no bardic badge; no dodging
of projectiles as he muses on the best way to note down a
soldier's dying breaths.

A poet picking morsels from the aftermath, the sad
survivors; analysing second-hand accounts for personal
embellishments, for misrememberings, for shy omissions.

The poet's aim: not to present for posterity the known
and indisputably dreary facts, but to cast the real events in an
unreal mould, and in so doing hope perhaps for accidental
truth.

AT MALDON

Muzzle-nuzzles.
Kisses on the nose.

Sugar-lumps suede-lipped from flattened palms.

A drift of dusty perfumes.
Barley-breath.

'Let the smiling circle of your shield
be the only face they fix upon.
    Let it twirl before you,
a bright umbrella dazzling,
for you to strike unnoticed from its rear.'

A soldier's ungloved hand
fanned to the disc of a horse's cheek
unbuckles the bridle.

'Let spear-tip be your tongue
protruding, taunting as it pokes
and waggles, till
they are affronted by its brash simplicity.
    Then let fly your word upon its point.'

3

A slap upon the rump,
the horses trotting hover-footed
to the lonely wood that hedges the field.
Huddled in among the mossy boles
with heads held low they peer out
blinking at the war-band's muddled ranks.

'Inscribe your arrow-shafts with marks of love
that, following their aerial ballet,
dig into the bosom of their beau.'

A boy in his rebuffed excitement
cooing to his blue-winged hawk;
tickled below the hard hook of its mouth,
its gold-ring gaze refuses to meet his.

Extending the upswing of his wrist
its light weight lifts,
is balanced on the brightness of the air,
allows the world to fall, to pivot,
and with the sharpness of its flight
positions the tree-top beneath it;
there to turn its back and pause and preen.

'When unabashed they rush to meet you
embrace them with broadsword,
with daggers caress,
till they wallow in the wetness of your kiss.'

In among the many: Eadric,
teenaged kinsman to the earl,
with tea-towels padding the sag
of his hand-me-down mail;
only half-heeding the speech's instruction,
of what is to be and not to be done,
tucks in his shirt and swallows his gum
to whisper his own words of comfort.

'Mum said to stand harder than oak,
so if they come on like a gale-force wind,
well, I shan't be so easily uprooted.'

Cresting the high banks
beyond the crowd:
the patchy yellow-blossomed gorse.

The ever-wind-blown willow,
backcombed branches
dipping to the weight of little birds.

'She said fear grows of ignorance,
how, unprepared, they'll be more scared of us.'

Seedcase fragments graining shady airs
garnish the conveyored river-top.

A gully deepens to the water's edge.
Sunlight through thin ripples
reddens flagstones.
Small black fish hold steady at the lip.

    'Stick with the prince
and with the fight
and do your best
and come back home again.'

Beyond the stream, the slope, the fringe of trees:
    the Viking horde —
who limber in the summer sun,
touch toes, check pulses, sip hot soup,
laugh at foreign jokes in foreign tongues.

    'Come blood and muscle-ache and grown men's screams,
there's nothing will make me doubt my mother's word.'

A great white horse, the sun
reflected off its silky flanks;
its tail's peroxide swish
as pallid skin-soft reins
are given over to the groom.
Led heavy-hoofed away.
Its big-eyed backward glance
beneath a flop of fringe.

And as the earl now backs himself
into the space reserved by his best,
upon the far shore:
                    a little man
detaching from the host
waddles to the waterside.

With the voice of a curlew
who finds his feet have dried fast into mud
he calls.

        'Dear neighbour,
long kept strange by a width of water,
see how hard we've worked to close the gap.
    One finger of wetness left to cross
till we can be together.'

The earl: secure within a knot of strength,
his colleagues from the club, his favoured few,
who check each other's costly gear,
re-cinching sculpted raw-hide over silk
zipped up at the back, behind
a chest-high screen of shields.

Old iron half-drawn from the scabbard
finger-greased with lightly scented oils.

'Do you think we'd step so far from home
if we were only looking for a fight?
    Our land expands, we'd like
to cut you in upon the deal. This is
a great investment opportunity.'

As one who slowly registers the soft persistent tapping
of a moth that bumps itself against a bulb, only now
does the earl squint towards the far bank;
                                    the little man
in his green-wool cream-lined fitted business suit,
little hands behind his little back,
pacing the shore in winklepicker boots.

    'A start-up fee, a bit of gold — a token, if you like.
You won't miss it.
    Bangled lords function better unshackled.
De-tag your lady's hole-punched ears.
Lift off the heavy lace that yokes her neck.
    And of those coins hard-bitten yet unused:
what good is gold kept hidden in a box?'

A foreign war-horde, cramped
upon a tuft of unkempt unloved land;
a bobble sprouted from the river-bed;
a morass — a swamp.

Behind: the furled umbrellas of their boats
parked neatly in a row,
high noses buried into ryegrass,
mooring ropes slung loose round crooked trees.

'A transaction of mutual good grace.
You pass over the money and we
provide an authentic receipt,
hand-printed and stamped.
   After which you can toddle off home
lighter-hearted, lighter-pocketed,
and with your integrity
on the right side of your skin.'

The channel that runs between them —
a thin limb of water, a steeply banked stream;
joined at each end to the wide neck of river
offering its body to the sea.

                              And here:
a single solid block of muscle-men,
from which lord Byrhtnoth
steps out, one pace forward,
leaving an earl-shaped gap in the leading edge.

  'Such a crowd to head out for so small a request
yet each of you wishing to fill your party-bags.
   Perhaps if the numbers were cut, but alas
my purse is still back at the castle.'

The broad-breasted river
puffed to capacity
now breathes out.

And as its top
is languidly raked off into the sea,
and as the sea-wind
doubles back to glide above the flow,
a peristaltic plug of water
bowls itself along the narrow stream.

   'But don't be too downhearted,
if it's metal that you want
we've enough here to weigh down your boats;
and it polishes as smooth as silver,
    if squinted at,
    in sunlight,
    from one eye.'

River-swell —
the flow sped up,
thickens the distance from shingle to surface.

A split meniscus overlaps the grass.
The water clouds with lifted silt,
darkening the gulf between the banks.

   'What's more we deliver direct,
secreted with care amongst your person
to ensure the last leg of your holiday jaunt
will not go unburdened.'

The river fumes, its flood of angry black
spills further outward, climbs the fording slopes,
covers up new cobbles with each surge.

Both armies have moved closer to the swollen river lips
— the spokesman backward-swallowed by his gang
— the earl re-slotted back into his block.

Just as matched magnetic poles brought close
reluctantly repel, so the armies
each pull away from the water's frothy brink.

Keyed-up they fidget along opposing banks;
a line-dance mirroring the bobs and shuffles of the other side,
while, every-so-often, carefully considered gifts
are exchanged across the divide.

Teasers, tasters, testing shots.

A sample-arrow, floated over trees,
a black scratch on the air
wobbled by the heavy breeze;
and a circular patch of men erect a temporary roof
to catch the bright barb as it falls.

A slimline javelin similarly pitched,
its flight-line cut from lower down the cone,
slides its point into the spongy wood,
    is plucked out
    inspected
    passed round
and duly returned.

The sea keeps at its lunar suck,
the stream subsides and settles,
waters clear, fish sneak back into the flow;
while Vikings pace like anxious pups,
eager to plunge but cautious,
pawing at the wavelets to be calm.

> Two armies, like two halves of an egg-timer,
> the ford a pinch in the glass, through which
> a few grains only at any one time may pass.

Slink-footed on the slip of stone,
the current tugging sidelong at their ankles,
three sea-farers try it on, are matched
by Wulfstan's three-man barricade.

A trio wedged into the narrow gully of the ford.
Aelfere and Maccus sporting knee-length shields
while Wulfstan, for all his bigness,
won't budge from between them;
waves his longest spear through the gap.

With neither side fool enough to get too close
six spear-heads jab and dip and glance;
hands inch backward down the hafts;
tip-control traded for extra reach,
like fishers casting nets and dragging them back
to cast each time a touch further.

Till the foremost Viking thrusts too far
and the lump-weight of his weapon pulls him
onto lucky Wulfstan's lifted point.

Two men linking arms with a third
heel-dragged from the river.

A spreading red ribbon
connecting body to water,
reeled out to the pull of the current.

Fish that sniff through the river's new essence,
gill-slits snagging on the rosy flow.

The bump of a spear carried backward downstream,
the scrape of its tip over gravel;
wet-wood pole poked upward as a swimmer's lifted head.

Re-ingested by his pack —
        the wounded soldier.
                        His replacement,
shunted from the body-press, the hole
into which the half-corpse disappeared —
        the little figure of the spokesman;

slows the sudden speed of his ejection,
brushes out the creases in his suit,
clears his throat.

'You will appreciate our disappointment
at this display of shoddy sportsmanship . . .'

Consider the shrink of a war-horde:
invisible diminution of clustered invaders,
sucked towards the vacuum of their boats.

' . . . negotiations will be halted
till conditions are improved . . .'

Black-body-flow, spread-fingered,
poured on board, packed in,
sails up, inflated,
dislocates them from the sticky mud.

' . . . fair play is all we ask, or else
send your men over here . . .'

An afternoon spent sailing up the coast;
the low white sun white-tips the choppy sea;
to pull in at a sleepy harbour town
without booking in advance
nor paying the mooring fee.

' . . . to sit, to go, it's much the same to us;
others may see more sense to our intent.'

A creep of men through moonlit streets,
through broken windows, knives through throats;
defenders in night-shirt and slippers;
a young girl's stifled sobs;
a snifter of smoke.

The wind is up with noon's hard heat.
Fast clouds stretch like putty, tear
and melt, and bloom from half-blued air;
the broad-beamed sun-star winking through the gaps.

Byrhtnoth's cobweb hair blows over his face.

Pursed fingers drum the pommel at his hip.

The shape of his army buckling backward.
A dent in the vanguard. The Vikings
watching, waving them further. Back and back,
blind-footed over furrows, hard ground to soft.
Bending their ranks to hold fast at the flanks,
thinned from a square to a crescent
its horns just touching the river;
leaves an open semicircle
centred by the ford,
into which:
        the Vikings,
having peered,
having taken survey of the site,
                now freely move.

Boot-splash after boot-splash.
Boots familiar to water.
Boots used to puddle-stomping unrebuked.

> *As a culture grows to fill the petri dish,*
> *bounded only by a brittle lip . . .*
> *As the compound substrate slots*
> *into the enzyme's active site . . .*
> *So, the designated space is occupied.*

A perfect half-moon, its flat to the bank.
A curve of faces, then
an empty strip of top-cropped grass,
then an answering curve.

It begins with crows,
black flecks against the blue,
like bits of bin-liner flapping on the wind;
like a mould spreading over the sky.
Two hundred pearl-black eyes,
black tongues in black beaks,
waiting for men to be meat.

It begins with an increase in noise,
as at the start of an orchestral interval:
the slow surge of coughing and audience chatter,
each new sound trying to out-sound the other;
as on a track as the train approaches,
what was mere hiss becomes a hurricane,
undirectional, the scream and suck of air,
earth-shake, fist-pounded shields,
a covering of chaos for each ear.

It begins with spears,
with javelins, arrows,
anything slender enough
to thread the gap, to darn
with a weaver's precision,
casting fast and low
to loop through the fringes and back.
But the sides are forever shifting
and the needles miss their marks,
the meshing uneven, entangled lines
down which the casters tentatively trace,
knives out to unpick the knots.

Waves beating up against cliffs.
Cliffs holding hard against waves.

The weight behind each water molecule;
each rush to scour more tissue from the rock.

The cliff-face weathered into jagged lines;
ceramic sharpness shattering the water.

And the bowmen are busy;
choice shots through the disarray
that missing one side-stepping may yet
stick in another behind.

And shields become cumbersome,
heavied by a hodgepodge of blunt-ended spines.

And somewhere in the early excitement
big-hearted baby-faced Wulfmaer is killed.

Beloved nephew of the earl,
in lifting his sleeve
to wipe away a creeping fringe of sweat
finds the liquid gumming his eyebrows
is thicker and hotter and redder than water.

And in pausing to ponder the source of the flow
a swung shard of sunlight sparks a fresh ache in his arm.

A brightness, opened up across his back.

The weakness in his thighs.

The wetness welling in his eyes.

He kneels
surrounded by a ring of light;
his deepening blush, so foolish with failure,
musters one last look towards the earl,

   'What was it they . . . ?'

who sees the big kid fall,

   'Why didn't you . . . ?'

a baggy man-sized lump upon the earth,

   'How now shall I . . . ?'

as their boot-soles roll the body over,
find Wulfmaer's worth already stripped;
so turn on old Byrhtnoth,
who gapes like a landed trout astounded
in its incapacity
as in its abundance of breath.

In comes: Eadweard —

who ambles into the closing gap,
his coolness masked by mild incompetence;
who trips and in his stumble sticks
his spear-head through the first man's jaw,
the body balanced upright on its point;
then swings his sword into the second man
so hard the blade snags on his pelvic bone,
and the man bows in acceptance of his fate.

Red-edged weapons wriggled free.
A nod from Eadweard to his earl

    — and on into the fight.

    'Like him.
    Like that.
    Do as he did.
    Kill as he killed.'

Byrhtnoth loosening his limbs
shakes off his old-man-mantle,
rediscovering the warrior beneath.

    'Fight with cunning, not with crudity.
    Think before you thrust.
    Let not your minds be mangled
by the butchery we're begged here to perform.'

Tucking the heel of his spear tight under his arm,
its tip to bob and waver
   eenie meenie miney mo
then jab and jab, as easy
as poking holes in plasticine.

  'Thank God for level-headed Eadweard;
when this is done he shall be dressed
with rows of shiny buttons, coloured string.'

    How fork-prongs press
    into a quartered lime;
    the ruptured membrane sag,
    the jet of juice.

  'He shall dine out with my daughter;
let her cleave to him as close
as burs caught in a sheepdog's coat.'

    How grapeskin splits
    with such little force;
    its dark flesh bulging
    outward through the tears.

  'He shall come round for afternoon tea;
let he and I sit out on garden chairs,
dunking shortbread, smoking small cigars.'

The undiscerning carry of his voice.
Its commanding tone that marks him
as prioritised for death.

In Danish corner-shops, between
the model boats and bow and arrow kits:
a rack of throwing-spears.
Each less than three feet long, lightweight,
the wood like a pencil hollowed of its lead.
Gaudy feathers glued to the heel
as lure to young collectors.
Each simple needle-nose protected
by a cube of cork.

 For practice.
 For sport.
 Made cheap.
 Disposable.

Without seeing where it came from, the earl
now finds one of these darts embedded
in the hard hide covering his chest,
stuck out rigid like a nail half-hammered into wood.

He knows it has not penetrated far,
knows it will come out with one good tug,
has not spied its delighted caster,
gangly, gap-toothed, rushing up behind.

A young Dane, in blond and blue,
who rams his shield into the butt
to drive the spear home.

22

Yet the bird-boned haft breaks into splinters;
the tip to strike no deeper than the sternum
before bending and springing back out.

Little more than a reflex,
a chance swing as he reels,
and Byrhtnoth's own spear travels
sideways through the soft white neck
of the Dane who stands aghast
at the popping open of his throat,
at the blood that floods his homemade armour,
brass rings tightly looped through leather,
into which the earl now stabs
the follow-up stroke:
bursts the breastguard open
like a nutshell neatly halved.

Byrhtnoth, as a beast bent over its kill;
panting; pondering —

touches at the pin-prick on his chest,

'A little thing; a badge, a half-hearted tattoo . . .'

the dribble of blood through the hole,

'. . . proof of the part I had to play in this . . .'

its wet soaking into his tunic unseen.

'. . . how I fared better than this clumsy fool.'

The boy on his back.
Blue eyes open to the sky.
Blond hair mingled through thick clover.
Dead-edged wounds quick-drying in the sun.

A flicker in the air,
a glint, a shimmer,
a second dart —

                thumps into Byrhtnoth.
The dull smack of its speeding stopped
as a cricket ball, pitched, and caught
in the leathery mitt of his midriff.
Its excess energy spent as heat and noise.

    High-velocity steel.
    A spiral-carved black shaft.
    Hand-plucked plumage,
    cut, split, trimmed,
    and sewn with silver wire.

An effect equal to its industry
as its polished umbrella-spike punctures the soft of his belly
and he feels the sickening sharpness of its tip
worming in his guts.

  'Don't look down.
  Don't move.
  Don't touch a thing.'

The gentled voice of Wulfstan's son,
stepping from the battle-haze,
kneeling in the half-tramped grass.

His tools laid aside
as he finger-dabs the zone
where stem becomes body;
the heavy heel of the dart
rested across his shoulder

   'A small hole.
    Very neat.
    Quite mendable.'

— as the point is eased out,
tossed away with a backhand flick.

   'Such craftsmanship.
    Such love.
    Such violence.'

A one-in-a-million shot for Wulfstan's son,
just one-in-one for the unlucky Viking
whose shock-wide mouth receives it with a gulp

   'Best leave it at that.
    Go easy.
    Get plenty of rest.'

— as the young man stands,
picks up his kit,
towels the blood from his hands,
then, harking to a nearby cry,
is smartly whisked away.

And the earl is left alone,
an invalid, a sick man,
pressing a gauzy bandage pad
over the leaky wound.

Byrhtnoth, using spear as walking-stick,
clutches at its steady upright line,
shrinks his tired weight to its wood
as the fight grinds on about him.

His ooze of pain becomes his sped-up life:
the pure white of his beard to pull at his cheeks;
the curl of his fingernails clawing to his palms.

Selective hearing dulls the battle's din:
the muffled talk heard through a rubber mask;
the upstair tenant's stomps upon the floor.

In the midst of which comes sharp the ring
of the river flowing clear over stones;
the heavy distant tolling of a church;
his own tintinnabulate whistle above the wind.

Still clinging to his staff as his sight closes in.
A creep of bright-rimmed blackness.
A misted tunnel-mouth.

Till nothing but nothing surrounds him,
an empty sphere neither lighted nor dark,
with him at its centre, a seed
still alive, still himself — unresponsive;
a mind re-learning how its body moves.

Till he senses his circle of calm has been breached,
feels for his sword-hilt;
    once veined in gold
    now black and cold.
The last drop of strength to close his fingers,
to draw the blade an inch,
to give air to its etchings —
        before a blow to his arm
breaks the bone, and the sword
snicks back in its scabbard,
as his strength is snuffed out,
as he slouches and waits.

'For the earl!
For Uncle Bert!
For daddy's old boss!'

The prancing of children at play on the lawn
while he snoozes
on moss and forget-me-not clusters,
a paperback over his face.

  'Is that you, little Aelfnoth?
What would I say to your mother
if you stained your smart new clothes?'

As carefree as sparrows
that spiral the trunk of an oak
they run rings round him
laughing too loud to take notice.
Their clumsy foot-patters.
The clack of their wooden swords.

  'Little Wulfmaer, be mindful;
a slip is all it takes for injury.
Go, leave me in peace.'

Still they ignore him,
go on with their skipping —

till tiredness takes them
and down they all fall
          in a heap,
      the two boys,
      the old earl,
      on the grass,
      in the sun.

And, like hens that peck and scratch
for white specks in the yard, so they
are hacked at where they lie.

As a bead of water traces its crooked course
across a slope of glass, pulled this way
and that as it joins with other stationary droplets,
grows larger, leaves a thinning trail, moves on —
so the whisper of the earl's last breath
describes a path through groups of fighting men.

And the sound of that sigh
plucks as it passes,
curling to the ears of those
who can decode the tones.

Some stiffen to its note,
their strength increases,
hafts and hilts gripped harder,
points and edges keen upon the scent
to kill and kill and kill.

                    While some
who sense the drag of death upon the air
with one step back put out of reach
the soft skin holding in their souls;
with weapons neatly sheathed they bow
to their assailants, turn
and walk away,
        then jog,
        then run.

Just as a designated driver
hangs about outside the theatre,
checks his watch from time
to time, so Godric, groom
to Byrhtnoth's great white horse,
lingers at the battle's back end.

To a soundtrack of distant clamour
he unpacks curry-comb, soft-bristled brush,
the thing-for-taking-things-from-horses'-hooves.

And as he polishes the silver trim,
and as the buffing-cloth turns black,
an impromptu crowd
breaks off from the battle
as cleanly as a shard of fractured flint.

A murmur carried cloudlike as they shuffle
like a string of refugees, their eyes downcast,
their war-gear gathered in their arms:

   'No use in seeing it through to the end
now the principle player is gone.'

As such Godric heeds
and mounts his charge,
ensuring its safety
in hastening their retreat;
sat so lordly in the saddle,
whited by his livery;
the horse to treat the blessed boy
no different from its master.

And in trotting from the scene he does not notice
his own wedge-shaped wake of deserters,
who take this stately exit as a cue,
sneaking back in silence to the town,
and who, without a parting word, peel off
from the group, each man to his home,
all front doors bolted, curtains drawn.

While Godric to the castle courtyard,
                                    goes alone,
    the horse into its box,
    the key put back beneath its stone.

No one to mark him.
Song from an open window —
the only sign of life;
a choirboy practicing his Sunday chants.

And in his lodgings Godric sits.
And in his lodgings Godric sleeps.

And Godric sweats his life into his job.
And Godric marries, loves, tries fatherhood.

And his grandchildren crowd him,
try to dig out his account of the battle.

   'O yes, I was there too.
I played my part
the day the Danemen came.'

And the nurse brings his food-tray,
empties the bedpan, changes the sheets.

   'Not my role to join in,
yet many men
owe their long lives to me.'

And the graveyard is packed out with silent spectators.
And his coffin is lowered.
And dirt is kicked into the hole.

   *   *   *

A farm boy ankle-deep in estuary mud.
His draw-string bag. His wooden whelking-spoon.
Eases the bend of his back. Considers the sea.

The white horizon's divisional line.
Flat white water. Flat white sky.
The salt-wind thickening his uncut hair.

Inclines again to his labours, his low skim
scanning for the stuck-out siphon tip,
then the quick dig, the measured scoop,
grit-clods thumbed from the grooves of the shell.

Tiddlers screwed back into the mud.
The others for his bag.
The horizon again.

As flat.
As white.

Yet grown now from the gap,
the split between water and air,
a row of twenty matchwood boats
with wide white handkerchief sails;
as still as cardboard cut-outs on the sea.

The farm boy at the water's edge, low tide,
washing the whelks, wetting the bag,
rubbing out the crust of mud built up between his toes.

One last glance at the advancing fleet,
no bigger than before,
no flap detected in their sails;
a dotted line of small white squares
down which to cut or sew or sign ones name;
and the boy heads home.

As a disturbed ant nest is still
a moment following the stick's deep thrust,
so the town hall as the meeting ends,
once the hammer is brought down,
once sentence has been passed,
is slow to stir.
                Yet soon
the people vibrate from their seats,
to pour through every orifice,
to spread in an unbroken wave out onto the streets.

And three men in particular,
pumped up by the emergent moot,
descend the town hall steps in synchrony;
their tripled shoe-tap striking stone,
granted space aplenty by the common-folk
that smoothly flow around them.

Aelfwine
      and Offa
           and Leofsunu.

Local heroes in the making.
Fine upstanding citizens.
Stood now in the emptying road,
beneath the clearing clouds of early day.

Time enough for a nip, a tonic
to boost prognosticated fortitudes.
Their brief invasion of the bar;
occupying strong positions
at the window-seat.

           Aelfwine
examining faces, each and every passer-by:
the quickness or else the ease of their step,
how they fumble with their front-door keys,
the force with which they shut themselves inside.

  'That won't be me.
I will not dig myself a hidey-hole.'

— as he lifts a thimble of port to his lips;
his chosen weapon,
his unsheathed knife,
blessed with two quick kisses,
pommel and point;

'I'll prove my noble line,
make papa proud, take pleasure
in the moral prospect of my death.'

— as he wends his path through warriors,
stooped low to spy a likely mark;
till he sticks an unsuspecting seaman,
burrows the slender blade into their side,
slid between the ribs to prick the heart;

'Even as the dead pile up around me . . .'

— as the dead pile up around him;

' . . . I'll not flee the field,
will not seek solace in my comfy home,
not at my daughter's wailing, nor my wife's;
no matter how hard she beats the cooking pot.'

— as he downs the sick-sweet syrup,
rises to ready his gear, is gone.

And then there are two.

                    And Offa,
to Aelfwine's example, salutes
with full-filled wine-glass raised;
then puts his eye to the cup's thin curve,
looks through its lens and sees red;

'Though we all know how words are limiting,
that strength is only lent through deeds
not by limp-wristed pats upon the back;
each foe cut down to prompt two further kills.'

— his long ash-spear to lead his charge,
to gather Danemen, skewered on its shaft,
who flop down lifeless as the pole retracts,
the wood made slippery with foreign blood;

'And even should our good lord fall . . .'

— as Byrhtnoth falls;

'. . . should his life be pricked and emptied out . . .'

— as the curtains of the fight are drawn aside
to reveal the earl, spot-lit, bewildered,
circled by a chorus-line of Danes;
                                    and who,
seeing how their song cannot be quelled,
buckles to their steady prompting,
sinks his heavy shell upon the grass;
his breath to seep into the soil.

'. . . there'll be no tears,
no trembled lips,
our ranks will grow as tight
as twisted rope;
such death to be the flame
that seals the ends.'

As a girl not wishing to stain her party frock —
As a swan that glides serene from mud-choked reeds —
   likewise the earl's horse, unmistaken,
   trots its silver trappings from the field.

 'For if the wrong thread is pulled
so the rope unravels.
   With the key-stone knocked out
so the construct collapses.'

So the battle-line is broken.
So the shield-defence is shattered.
And like a bun of consecrated bread
the army tears in two.

   'And should I ever meet the man that baulks . . .
   And should he swear he never had a choice . . .'

And Offa issues from the ale-house,
winces to the bright white morning light,
blindly sets his foot upon the road.

And then there is one:

          Leofsunu,
who pours his second cup of thick black tea;

 'No. No, be well assured
I'd not falter, nor would I flinch.'

— whispered as he warms his hands;
the blood to pink his fingers,
make them quick;

   'To die out on the field is better
than to limp back lordless
with my tail between my toes.'

— as he levers a leaf from between his teeth,
flicks a gobbet of flesh from his wrist;

   'To throw my weight on enemy iron,
its penetrative hardness, its tincture, its tang,
would be my comfort, my homecoming.'

— as he skips and twirls into the fray
a spear extending from each hand,
a grey whirr of blades like a blender on full;
so his foes are chopped and spun aside,
flung from the merry-go-round.

   'Yes. Yes, that would be homely.
And no one could brand me as idle
if counted as one of the dead.'

— as he pushes in his chair,
scatters the tip they left for him to leave;
small roundish wafers of metal
falling like seed upon stone.

And then there are none,

                  except Dunnere:
stalwart owner of this drab establishment,
who shuts up shop now they're gone;

   'And what if I should see my loyal patrons polished off?'

— as he stacks stools on the counter,
lets the blinds down, locks the doors;

   'And what if they should see me shy?
having served so stoutly all these years.'

— as he slips into a slinky leather two-piece;
laces long-heeled boots about his calves;

   'To see their faces sag expressionless,
will I be sorrowful?
will fury buoy me up?'

— as he lifts his granddaddy's sword from its red-velvet case.
   Its warmth of heavy metal.
   His unaccustomed grip.
Away from which the war-scarred edges dip.

   'What youngsters did you open in your day?'

A tatty cloth with which he dusts away
its pitted powdering of rust,

'Can I be sure such weaponry still works?'

and tucks it underneath his overcoat,
stepping from his pantry door
into the midst of gathered battle-crew.

        Here, the master cobbler,
in his mirror-polished linseed-lacquer shoes,
newly soled and stitched for the day's event;
his wooden-handled awl, his ball of wax;
the one stowed in his sock, a last resort,
the other fondly squeezed within his fist
as on he walks

        beside the local quack;
bloodletter to his trusting customers;
who's left his leeches swimming
in their jar, while he regresses
to his school days, the dissection table;
corpses arrayed in stages of undress;
recalls his quickness with the knife
and how to strip a man down to his bones;
crude medicine but worthy of review
as on his other side

                              the hushed librarian;
who's reinforced his coat with hardback books;
who's given up his date-stamp,
left behind his abecediarised displays;
exchanged the vicious cut of paper
for the hand-cupped whisper of the sword;
his pacifism put on hold to join in
with the throng

                        where spears predominate;
points high above the pseudo-soldiery,
their stems like underwater weeds
that sway to the swell of the march.

This ragamuffin mob in fighters' garb;
each man's own idea of unchecked uniformity;
who've raided their antiques drawers,
their unvisited museums.

    Bronze age.
    Iron age.
    Zirconium dioxide.
    Diamond-dust.

Sharp edges can forever be re-sharpened,
so long as there is blade enough to cut.

As such they go down to their deaths
all masked in bygone bravery,
all swearing, boasting, claiming
they won't be the ones to blench.

And some get lucky in the mess of pre-production,
while the army is moulded and stretched,
in elbowing eagerly through to the front.

A smattering of extras rubbing shoulders with their lords.

Awaiting the whistle,
the lady's hanky to be dropped.

So they may lead the charge.

So they are seen.

So they fall first.

As vegetation rots and is compressed
through lapsed millennia
by successive layerings of decay,
till all its goodness is squeezed out
and it blackens as it flattens into coal,
so bodies freshly fallen are packed down.

Beginning as an awkward bumpy cover for the grass
they soon become new ground.
Nestled so close identities are lost,
their limbs all locked,
their blended bloods;
an indiscriminate plateau.
The intermittent strata of the dead
through which the patter of the world above
vibrates so softly,
many dainty feet,
sending messages of comfort, to remind
that they are not wholly forgotten,
that they will be joined before long.

Concealed within the press of the Saxon crowd:
Aescferth the archer, a lad from The North,
who, by birth, should not be here at all;
who tip-toes from cover to cover
as though the men were a fence of thickset trees
that every-so-often lift up their roots,
shift forward and replant, to hold and fight.

Aescferth: on an exchange scheme, part of a pax
between regions the reigning families have devised
to swap their sons, as insurance
against unscheduled skirmishes.

These people aren't his people.
This fight is not his fight.
Well within his rights to sneak off,
to thumb a lift on the northward road
to the home he has not seen for half a life,
explaining to his parents, now estranged,

    how things did not work out,
    how complications arose,
    how he had to get away.

                 Yet when
his foster father over breakfast says — *let's go*,
he closes up his book of household tales,
uncrosses his ankles, and goes.

    A bracer finely broidered with his name.
    Spare string coiled in the pocket of his shirt.

Now peeking out, now dipping back
behind his unprotesting living shields,
he calculates quadratic arcs —
one root: himself, the other: his mark.

A momentary straightening,
a twang no louder than a peg pulled off a rain-wet washing line,
and down again he ducks.

No need to watch the elegantly drawn parabola.
No time to chalk a hit, nor curse a miss.
The follow-up routine is just the same:

A furtive peep
An arrow nocked
The pull
The pluck
Repeat

And in the lulls that come
when space is given as the bodies drop
and hand-to-handers momentarily retreat
    to catch a breather,
    whet worn edges,
    mop hot brows:
                    Aescferth
nips out for munitions,
tugging at the arrows stuck
like lonely stems of wheat among the slain.

Likewise, other archers creep
from either side, with backs bent low
to comb for pickings,
squabble over brightly-coloured flights,
                    or else,
as Aescferth, exchange an occasional nod
with strangers in their searching.

Till the quivers are restocked,
and the bowmen backstep,
discreetly hid amid the plenty,
allowing dead-man's-land to close back up.

The shield-line of Vikings, hinged
between the fighters' boots
and the bruise-backed grass,
so that when their line is weakened
they simply flip down flat, ready
for new men to ratchet forward,
spring-loaded from behind.

Till lanky Eadweard, frustrated
by this nigh impenetrable guard,
steps clear across the woody blockade
to wade alone among the enemy.

> 'If we can't beat them back into their boats . . .
> If we won't budge a foot-space further . . .'

The pendulous swing of his sword,
its slow clean arc that parts the men below.

> *As easy as a spawn of bubbles*
> *patted flat in the bath,*
> *likewise their bodies*
> *wink out of existence,*
> *only for more bubbles*
> *to slide in, filling the holes.*

> 'If I restrain from bending to their blows . . .
> If I keep their attentions fixed on me . . .'

As Eadweard grows weary, overwhelmed
by the onslaught's endlessness,
so he is hewed from base to brow,
and, at length, lies like firewood
piled up about their feet.

His object nonetheless achieved,
his bit of damage done,
in breaking up the Viking war-machine,
in opening its edges from within.

And many Saxon soldiers take
the proffered opportunity
to get in deep,
shooting themselves singly into the splits
to rip fine tunnels through the innards of the horde.

A band of childhood friends,
kept in a cluster, fighting back to back,
exit from one side to enter the other;
moving like a spinning-top
they hum across the blurred divide.

This is their playground, their backyard.
Now the rains have stopped,
now the sun has dried the land,
they've left off moping in their beds
and gathered up their toys to romp outdoors.

At their touch:
intricately decorated shields are cloven with a hollow pop;
armours are unravelled at the seam to unshell blushing
    occupants.

Hard-hats clack like castanets.

Belts spill open with full-bellied sighs.

And on the band of friends keeps spinning,
swept up in the musical frenzy, their swords
spring out, rebounding to their coiled energies.

Offa watches from his vantage point,
his dead-men mound,
finger-veils his eyes from splintered light
to trace the progress of this team,
this food-packet entering into the fight;
and how the Vikings work it,
rolling it from cusp to cusp,
its brittle casing gnawed at till it cracks,
till it is tenderised inside;
a fleshy bolus nudged into position
    and swallowed
                and gone,
                    and Offa
swings his gaze to search for something else.

A hallowed patch of corpses —
covered up by criss-crossed limbs.
    A gleam of gold.
    A wisp of white.
    A familiar face.

'Our promise was the homecoming parade.
How with the top down, side by side, we'd wave.
    And the crowds would adore us,
would scream our names,
would swoon and faint and fall as we passed by.'

Descending from his perch into the fray,
which like water rises past his waist —
which like weed curls tight about his legs
so that he needs to hack a path
— so that he has to beat the water back,
slashing at the wavetops as he pushes through the flow.

'Our promise was that every wound inflicted
on your body would be dealt as well to mine.
    How we would lie down, side by side, and wait,
for the skies to fade to black,
for our souls to drain and dissipate,
mingled in the soils of our land.'

Offa tramples.
Offa kicks and shakes away
the blades and barbs
invading his personal space.

Like flies they scatter.
Like flies they buzz back.

A glittery swarm;
a hive-mind set to pester,
that neither knows nor wants to stay away.

Till Offa's pipes are cut,
and the big machinery of his body settles;
    the pistons flushed of air,
    the fuel-tanks dry,
    the sockets clogged.

 'Our promise was to never be apart.
From the moment our mothers laid us side by side
we understood
that one should not have to endure
without the other,
that hale and heartiness means nothing
if at last you come home empty-handed.'

Sprawled — as though he crawled
and with the last dregs of his strength stretched out;
as though they left him, saw no reason
for the final blow; or stood and watched
in wonder at the purpose of his reach,
as broken fingers curled to boot-tip
of another corpse, who could have been
a man of some importance;
or could as likely have been anyone.

As a tanker, got up to full speed:
no matter how many little boats
kamikaze into its bows
it keeps on coming,
as the Vikings keep coming.

As a fluid fills the space it is assigned,
so the seamen fill the vacuums formed
when one of their number is felled;
a new man welling smooth into the gap.

As a busy kitchen table, topped
with half-licked spoons,
with crusted mixing bowls;
regardless of how often it is cleared and scrubbed,
so soon, unnoticed, unseen,
it becomes unaccountably cluttered once more.

No matter how many of their shields are broken into kindling.
No matter if their armour hangs in tatters from their skin.
No matter how deep the spear is pushed to pierce the gloomy
    membrane of their soul.
No dint can be made in the oncoming force.

As athletes who practise for hour upon hour
so that when the day comes all their efforts ring true;
little care for the crush of opponents defeated —
all that matters to them is the win.

As such they are professional.
As such they put full pride into each kill.
Are keen to spread that sense of joy they feel.

Hand in hand, with friend, with foe,
they alternate to form a human ring.
And when the ring constricts their bodies clash.
And when the ring dilates their fingers strain to keep a hold.
And weapons nose and wave within the circle's inner space.
And when they break and turn around
the battle is resumed.

Yet, with all the big names gone,
there's little cause left for their concern.

        Till Wistan joins activities.
Then the Vikings stand astonished
at his graceful step, his mastery;
the fearlessness worn lightly on his face;
his body-buzz; his aura's lucid edge.

With smiles, with nods, with one-hand-claps
they praise the deft precision of his blades,
and how the metal seems to sit so weightless in his grip,
allowing him a triple-kill
of men delighted to be slain with such unerring skill,
before the others converge to cut him down.

As farmers sometimes stand as the day ends,
as the light turns gold and shadows lengthen,
to look across the field they've tried to clear,
at the work still left to do;
so the Vikings stand and look
and lean and nudge and point and strategise,
and unwrap cold-beef butties,
and divvy up the workload as they snack.

In the temporary calm the landed crows
fold up the newsprint rustle of their wings
to trampoline between the corpses,
stalk the new-laid ridges of the dead.

Beyond: a line of Saxons
like a line of paper dolls; or like
a seam of sacred ashes over which
the Viking raiders must not step.

The crows become black crosses,
the evening breeze to raise them
back into their holding pattern,
as the string of soldiers closes in.

And as the Saxons close they overlap,
the remnants of their vanguard thickening;
men in old rags, sandbag-bodied, rods
stuffed up their shirts to keep them straight;

for whom the Vikings open up,
receiving them as hair receives a comb.
The Saxons: slotted in among the Danes.
One mass of intermingled soldiery.

> *Like a grain of grit within a shoe.*
> *Like a swallowed wasp that won't stop stinging*
> *from the inside out; all hope*
> *of its escape abandoned, it goes on,*
> *doing all that it has left to do.*

'Pick out the fattest Viking you can find.
Then count to twelve before you tag me in.'

Two brothers, twins:
Oswold and Eadwold;
their ripe red cheeks,
their tight white teeth,
their blazing big blue eyes.

'Hold hands so I won't lose you in the crush.
Swap places so they can't tell who is who.'

When Eadwold flounders Oswold hoists him up,
dusts off the grass-seed,
kisses bruises,
and on with the fight they go.

   'I'll tidy your room for a year if you make the first kill.'

When Oswold falls back it is into Eadwold's arms,
who pinches the blood from his brother's eyes,
replaces the sword in his palm.

   'I'll never again use your books without asking.'

   'I'll never again call you names.'

As easy as riding a see-saw:
one lifts the other up when he is down.
A matter of balance more so than of strength.
Till their timing gets skewed
and they go down together,
helpless to each other where they lie.

Here an old master picks through the mess,
draped in a graduate gown, his sword
a bright ruler, ready and eager to punish the upstarts;
dismissing their childish attacks with a swish of the wrist.

And though the hot vibration of each stroke,
whether taken or made, digs at his strength,
drags at the frayed strings of his tired old soul,
his mind remains as hard as the iron
he angles through the cracks of each assault.

'Here's a pretty thing amidst the grim-faced commoners:
a lordly skull with the skin still on it;
the rest of him uglied by tramples of ignorant feet.'

Like a hound that growls beside its owner's grave —
once the pieces of his prince have been sniffed out
he cannot be coaxed away,
neither with treats nor with taunts.
Starved into translucence
with no lustre to his coat,
the teeth yet retain their toughness,
all care rerouted to the aiming of each bite.

'Don't worry if they say you were too proud,
or that your best was not near good enough;
we'll get our go at winning next time round,
and let no man think we were ever soft.'

The niggle of a half-remembered thought.
An itch unreached between the shoulder-blades.
A sculptor blank-faced at his marble block.
                    As with these things:
it is merely a matter of patience;
of finding the right tool for the job;
of drawing out the shape within the stone.

Till his energy's so totally exhausted
all he can do is lie and watch and wait,
the eyeballs twitching fierce in their sockets,
the sergeant-major of his mind
that rages at his muscles to respond.

But there's no strength left even to convulse,
nor whimper as the spears are driven through.

In silence he slides out through the holes
their polished points have opened to the earth.

So, one man hits another
and the other hits him back.

And if the second man refuses to retaliate
the first man hits him harder.

> As two dogs that go on scrapping,
> till a hand braves a collar to drag them apart;
> but they'd go right on scrapping if they could.

The beat of the battle.
The tick-tock of clockwork.
The perpetual cardiac pulse.

And another man
named Godric fights
for everything he has
or has not loved;

who wallops men unconscious with his shield;
who swings his spear so hard its tip breaks through
    the speed of sound —

a whistle,
a bend in the breeze,
a shock-wave ghosting the arc of its path
as it strikes foreign armour
to slice through like water
to let what the armour held back pour out through the split.

His actions noted by his allies,
who know him by name, and who
are well acquainted with the battle's histories.

   'Is that not the man who played on his fiddle
and lured half our army away?'

As this Godric like a swallow dips
between the moving hatchwork of blades
and spins on his heel, on a breath, in the air,
to shoot back down the line with arms outspread,
scything through a dozen Danish necks.

'Is that not the man who slit the earl's throat
then rode his prized white horse to market
and sold it for dogs' meat and glue?'

As this Godric steps
between his critics
and a volley from the Viking bows;
and the arrows strike his skin as soft
as handcast stems of straw.

    'Is that not the man . . .'

As this Godric's cheeks are wetted,
first with tears, then with blood.

    '. . . who smuggled coastal maps and tidal charts . . .'

As this Godric is knocked down
by a blow to the head
intended for somebody else.

    '. . . and cut new keys to give our town up to the Danes?'

As he is buried under bodies newly dead,
and hears the rumour of the fight above,
the rhythm of hit after hit,
as calm, as constant, as familiar
as the soft wet tap of rain upon a roof.

    *   *   *